BELLOWING IN THE COMMON

Bellowing in the Common

Karl Petersen

Regent College Publishing
Vancouver, Canada

Bellowing in the Common

First printing by Regent College Publishing, an imprint of the
Regent College Bookstore,
5800 University Boulevard, Vancouver, B.C. Canada V6T 2E4

E-mail: bookstore@regent-college.edu
Website: www.regent-bookstore.com
Orders toll-free: 1-800-334-3279

Printed in the United States of America

Cover design by Vivian Law

Canadian Cataloguing in Publication Data

Petersen, Karl, 1955–
Bellowing in the Common

Poems.
ISBN 0-88865-432-4 (Canada)
ISBN 1-57383-140-9 (U.S.)

I. Title.
PS8581.E8412B44 1999 C811'.54 C99-910423
PR9199.3.P452B44 1999

Contents

Foreword

Karl Petersen comes from the same geographical and spiritual region as Theodore Roethke and Raymond Carver. His subjects are in the city: tenants and neighbours, who live on the edge of coping. It is subject-matter which will align him emotionally and thematically, with the common men and women who are the soul of his parish.

His kingdom of heaven is blue-collar, and these are mournful and musical meditations, human and ironical laments, bellows even at the shared predicaments in the streets and indoors, where tenants and neighbours inhabit the top floors of paradise and basements of hell, here, in the grey blue boundaries of the soul known as the West Coast.

The *Bellow* is to make contact with the bigness and the eternal—for Karl Petersen is also a wanderer with a sense of adventure and mission. A many hundred mile kayak expedition lies well within his undertaking. The conjunction of big physical stretch and the spiritual is the other link between those who have travelled this far across the earth to be transformed.

—George McWhirter
Professor of Creative Writing
University of British Columbia

Acknowledgements

A person's achievements are seldom totally their own. Never have I found this to be more true than in bringing together this body of poetry. I'd like to thank the many who have made it possible and whose influences are inevitably woven into the fabric of the work. It was Loren Wilkinson who first encouraged me in the belief that talents long latent and ignored could be revived, often simply waiting in hope of a resurrection.

Thanks go to George McWhirter whose uncanny eye and steady empathy led me through the throes of writes and rewrites, who showed me how to find a gem in any rubble heap. Also, the students of writing workshops at the University of British Columbia consistently helped me to see new dimension and possibilities in my work.

I'd finally like to thank the many friends and passers-by who may have unwittingly inspired these lines, and who may or may not recognize themselves in them. I assure you, I only wish you grace and immortality.

—Karl Petersen

1

Proclamations

Antiphony

Listen,
the ocean drone:
crescendo, diminuendo, retardando,
the faltering but never-failing tune
even the untrained ear can hear:
the rush,
the cascading castanets of stone
down a kelp-fretted score,
and silky-tongued phrases fading,
fold on fold, rolling on.
The chant murmers, *vesper light*
in tones of many hues,

as on the bank you lie
rapt in your sleeping bag.

Batons of fir penetrate a dark heaven
and stir the sky deep into the sea song:
microbes spray the firmament
and pulse phosphorescently on assigned lines
in time to the universal antiphony.

And you look up
from your down chrysalis, waiting
for the moment to emerge
and join in the hallowed dance
like a naked fool on the breakers.

Island Seduction

Sea lions of this island cove
mock me, will you? Come then, laugh
and tell me your secret,
share your game.

Island water, break
over my pebbled heart, rattle me
until the dead wood rises in a froth,
jostle me
like these empty sulking hulls,
from my stays, roil me
till I hear water speak,
untether me
so I sigh and rock
to metered passages.

Brush me, silken wings of gulls
with dawn's concupiscent light,
unshade me
while stagnant senses wake.

Nootka

Our heads and busts protrude
from kayak cockpits, ocean gophers,
we bob on
wrapped in a skin of fiberglass
faith.

Pivoting in our holes, we see
Escalante's sand stranding
a mile behind, in and out
of view over the rolls of surf, fading
with each press of paddle blades
against Nootka Sound water.
The land abandoned, floating free,
our imaginations rhythm
to the Sound of Nootka.

Seven hours pass,
the bow finally grinds
up the stone landing
and we are shore bound
again. The Sound
in our shoulders,
tangled in the sinew
of our arms, our backs. Its
laughter, fury, the play
of its body's contours
murmur in our memories.

Surf has mottled my cap's bill,
invisible particles of sand
grind in my Swiss knife
and a stone has a dent wedged
in the skin of my heel. Nootka

has breathed flush in our faces,
sketched us with its light:
patterns of sandal straps,
red knee caps
and bandana lines. Everything
about us speaks its name: Nootka.

Escalante

This water,
how it surfs and expands
incessantly across rock-calloused beaches
and 8 a.m. suns cedar boughs
on the opposite side of the sound.
This morning
an onion sky peels
inhibitions away, forgetting,
speaking: yours unending.
                                        Oh God,
it's been so long. I cannot cry
or laugh,
I cannot take this ocean in.

Whaling

You play the waves
of archipelago pathways
in arches black on white, Killer
they call you, I call you Worship,

rising at first light to release
sighs of vaporous praise,
pent up ecstasy sprayed
sky-bound from the deep;

your pliant fin genuflects
a glint of reverence, and a wake
whispers through the dawn
guiding the dull and disquieted

to a far off Light; big Worship
plunging again for fresher treasure
and erupting nose first to the sun
in one great lunge of praise.

The Word

A dense scent descends
in the after-rain air, wetted
by the wind-sent west word,
gathered and heard
in the girth of garden life.

Flecks of granite glistening
bellow it near the hedge's end,
a warbler's soliloquy
speaks it through the cool
before dusk drops the curtain.

It dances and pirouettes
through long dawns,
in the spindle legs of puddle striders,
weightlessly relevé,
six-stepping across stagnant stages
that ripple with the reverberant word.

Across the lane old Trudy putters,
muttering praises, lost
beneath arching spikes of bloom.
She winces toothless grins
at the word in wonder,
as a dog's snout roots for it in the dirt.

The evening curtain draws,
every beast, rock and primrose
shudders and is still
at the end and beginning of day
when all that is heard
is the salient word: silence.

Revolution

The wind came last night,
the fir out back snapped like gallows
hanging head to the ground,
the forty-year grape trellis thrown down too;

in one breath
it took the plum tree,
severing my memory at the main branch,
and turned it for another shape,

like a revolution leveling
forgets old fixtures, looks only ahead,
harrowing in my mind
a sad soil, such long clay.

Travelers in the Trees

awaking to the still of pre-dawn,
there is flocking in the trees
outside, birds touching down
bring tales of distant lands,
reveling in strange tongues, loud as
foreigners in a backpackers' haven,

and I only imagine
the miles and trials weathered,
the breadth of life they tell of

turning, I stare inescapably
at my clock's clipped wings
(they're wrong about time flying) how
they circle in a whiteness that is not sky,
beating out the rhythm of my day:
    shower and breakfast,
    bus, nine to five and
    back home, crashing
    on the couch while the sun sets,
    three months to Christmas break

and I feel the walls and want,
want none of this,
to join the travelers in the trees,
but I am inside
listening out to their tales,
my tongue alien to their world

Getting the Job Done

a discordant muse meanders
through my drawer,
scrambling files of daily resolutions,
jobs
undone
undoing me

this enchanting muse craves flesh
and bones,
or black and white, at least, ink
on a page

but the thought does not fit
around the three-fourths nut on the Ford
or the handle of my garden spade,
it confounds
the loud gasp of my wallet
and will not grab the boss's fancy,
but will not let me go
until it gets job done
until it waves and quietly lets pass by

Betrayed

the tulips came and went
he knows by the petals clinging
to a ripened knob on the stem,

but when, where was
the usual warm upheaval
of his crusty spirit? he
recalls no intoxicating,
pungent earth long latent
coming again like old love in
a sudden wave through the brush,
no orbiting of differential sun patches
across corners forgotten in his studio;

the months have passed through
a spring that was never there,
leaving him betrayed; yet

he wonders by the tulip petals:
she may have come,
perhaps stronger than before,
lingered and left,
while he, the unfaithful one
was absent,
growing cold to her touch.

Father's Day

Picking at brunch plates
atop The Landmark Hotel,
you and I gyre in clouds,
carried on the steady hum
of our motorized cafe carousel,
Vancouver's streets
carved tick-tack-toe below,
spinning out of sight
then back again
as we make the one hour round.

The closest we get to talking
of fathers is: they were both
struck with heart attacks. One
after seeing his girl turn sixteen;
the other, seeing his boy become a man,
turned and dropped, drifting
into the wide blue,
leaving us to wonder
when this attack on our hearts
will come full circle again.

Smorgasbord on Broadway

A vase of wooden tulips and angel's wings,
a bowl of ceramic fruit decked
on an oak table at the Country Living Store.

Western Lighting, Ltd., stocks a window-full
of "Canada's largest supply" of lamp shades.
(We have enough shade, thanks anyway.)

Finn's blazers for two ninety-nine, and don't they
know we don't wear suits in Kits? Haven't moved
for six months from the front display.

Twizzle Hair Salon looks busy
cutting one lady's curly, brown hair.
(Where do the straight-hairs go?)

Tokyo Joe's shows plastic *udon* and *maki sushi*,
while a Black Lab waiting on leash outside
chews a soggy stick of twisted bread.

Leftovers

Before the first snow falls
starlings raid Rybaski's tree for
rotting apples, some ornaments
left for these Christmas waifs,
dangling like so many dull suns
in a west December sky dank
with remembrance. They bob
pick and peck the last daylight
breaking from the soft orbs.

Raven Squawk

below the timberline
over a firred hollow
a raven's squawk rattles
a heavy breast
and guttural chords
flutter coned tops
and down
pierce a misty sleep
stirring underwood

Landed Immigrants

5:30 AM, I'm curled
in night's dark shell,
sleep's warm down still around,

and in the tree by my window,
morose in their shades of grey,
the spoilers, nest robbers, who
have pushed out more desirables—
robins, wrens, real songbirds—
free-loaders on the first
merchant ships from England:
a band of starlings
starts tuning up for a morning gig;

encroaching on
my hallowed piece of ground,
they squat at my nest's edge,
peck at my shell,
trying to suck me out
before the night's full incubation...
too late, it's done.
I lie exposed to the band,
a floppy sleepless mass,
undone,

seething,
damn immigrants!
before it hits that
they are landed here like me,
singing a different tune
in the same Creator's overture.

Palm Sunday

He rides ungainly,
legs draped
dangling over the donkey's sides,
lilies clip past his toes,
and his body sways
with the beast's uneven strides,
while branches wave homage
from the crowd
lost in cries of "Save us!"
from what they do not know.

Someone catches
the flicker of Roman shafts
atop David's city citadels,
and sends up cursings on them
in the name of God.

He nears the city,
the crowd grows,
and he knows
he is alone.

He weeps
and voices fade, the crowd blurs
through tears, and he feels
the timid beast's coarse hair,
hears small hooves clicking on stone,

then through the gates
into the heart of the city
of generations of mothers
who have dreamed over babies' faces
of what they did not know.

This Sunday
before the Friday called Good,
the drama's replayed
by children in prim dress
down the nave with waving palms
to triumphant "Hosanna" songs,
white belled blooms spraying the altar.

I wonder why the celebrating,
why the yearly partaking
in the grand delusion,
and like every year
my spirit turns,
does not dance with theirs,
the chorus mocking my dissonance.

The pastor's voice recedes,
and I only hear the small hooves,
see the lilies in the brush of his feet,
the bend of his head.
Then I understand, and cry,
because I'm there
with the man
who was alone upon the ass.

In the Eyes

I like the way you talk
making new words
like "indifficult"
and "another wear"
for underwear,
and the way you say "no"
from the hidden metal inside,
the way it's all there
in your eyes, eyes
that ride
in the vast vocabulary
of a mid-spring sea.

First Day in Japan

I say nothing
only watch the signs rising
monolithic-like above narrow streets

or splattered on windows
like finger paints (I think I saw a tree

or boy running maybe) a script
of cross stitch, needles and thread
hemming everything in

and meaning something
to those with the decoding power.

Billboards with round feminine faces
smile down and speak sweet nothings,
touching nothing in me.

Not Here in Japan

It's still only November 9 in Kumamoto,
slouched on my apartment box tatami mat
with a collection of Robert Frost in my hand.
I put on Handel's Messiah
to escape the rain, the stuffiness, the
foreign manners and words,
and drift content with the familiar chords
to Christmas back home in Lynden,
singing Handel in a mass choir,
surrendered as a youth in it
along with the dark-suited elders, their
black bow ties burrowed in their beards
as we sing, fixed on
the conductor's red face and
bone-white baton, crescendoing
and diminuendoing, like waves
the Messiah soaking into my marrow,
pushing out the winter rains.
And hearing Handel, I'm there,
not here in Japan. Then

in my hand I read Frost,
"we found out that it was ourselves
we were withholding from our land of living,"
and I'm suddenly back in Japan.

On the other side of the wall
the neighbor lady talks on the phone,
truck fumes are rising from the street
through the humid air,
and I lift myself slowly from the tatami mat
that has pressed the pattern of its grass fibers
indelibly into my elbows as I sat.

Susuki

I see Japan
whenever I see *susuki* grass
growing along most paths there,
in autumn, tasseling out
as braids of golden lace
in strands fanned on strong stems,
adjusting with the wind, bending
light patterns on the road.

I see gracious heads nodding
bowing, deferring power,
plumed phrases
and polite inquiries
echoing down the road.
They jostle in bunches,
their heads swirling opaquely,
whispering in the 5 PM sun.

Bright fans for dance
find their form from them,
invert one to shape
the sweep of a temple roof,
or hold a tight braid of one
straight in your hand
and find the bell rope of a shrine.

There, one wild stem
at the fringe sways out,
then whirls back
to balance the bunch
in perfect pitch.

Heaven on Earth

I've pre-tended my den carefully,
my little peace of paradise:
        a CD player, book shelves and TV
        judiciously set around, with a small table
        and cup of tea resting uneasily
        on the arm of my easy chair,
        a couple of potted plants.
One room

I keep in order, clear of junk mail,
socks and dirty plates. But out from one corner,
from the green palm, like a snake
slithers a long brown tendril
across my den carpet, a runner
come just to remind me
not to get too cozy.

Like Margaret Avison

I read a Canadian poet once, Margaret Avison, who unfolded mysteries to me. I wanted to be like her, to have something of me preserved for the good of another.

So at the library I searched out a periodical that held some of her work from early years: the catalogue said, Special Collections. Must be really something, I thought, and moved eagerly, her lines pulsing my veins, as I threaded a crooked labyrinth, three wrong turns, up to the top floor, down a windowless corridor to a high stark-walled room, no books in sight.

A grim-faced special librarian slipped me a green request form, then slid parsimoniously through a secret door in back, my little paper tightly in hand, and retrieved the sought out item: thin and black. At last, I reached, she pulled: "You can't take this out, have to read it here."

I obeyed, browsed awhile, and asked for a copy machine to have some gems to take away with me. A "copy request" form skidded my way: yellow.
"You can't copy this book yourself. We do it."
"Why the fuss?" I queried.
"Because these books are meant to be preserved."
"No thanks," I said and walked away, my passion for posterity dissolving, wondering again if I could end up bound here like Margaret Avison.

What Will It Take

Green rose bud,
your tough togetherness
that once allured
leaves me now so often alone,
wondering what reach
it takes (not mine)
to disclose you
or what hollow lying
under your brambled ground
will patiently woo an opening.

Not Alone

Waves of hair
lap
down your cheeks, move
with the tired cadence
of your voice
        swells he resists being carried on
        into your need,
        a spaciousness he could nestle down in.

Several passers through
have landed on your porch and
skirmished inside a fortnight or two,

and he wonders how you would take him in,
who else he would find inside.

October Lent

the sun angles low
at four PM today already
casting a yellow hue
over the garden
and stroking cool
across the face

(like a good-bye)
the maple's green rustling
has become a dying
rattle in the breeze
its unleaving leaving me
in wonder of

how the apple tree stoops
its life spent out
in great red drops
to satisfy those
who gather and store

how is it?

like my first roast duck
that fell along the swelling creek
folding from full-bodied flight
with the rush of gun powder
mingling in the sudden quiet

how one's end is another's beginning

like the maple
ablaze with dying
shaking red and orange

now shedding its stained mantle
dazzling dizzying down
as a fury of flames
flung around me
in a moment
that caresses a familiar sadness
and quickens delight

Window Watcher

sits where sun
                        spreading
        through the round morning
sycamore
can smack him
full in the face,
        where blinding
it can wash him
clear of day
kept just beyond the pane

A Bicycle With a Black Wicker Basket

Early December
outside the coffee shop stands
a bicycle with a black wicker basket
with mandarin oranges. A woman
in a skirt and lavender sweater
shuffles quickly by hunched,
reaching futilely for the coat she forgot.
A man stands
sucking squint-eyed
at the butt of a cigarette
for the warmth at the end of a long drag,
smoke wisping into the air,
as snow flicks across his face,
the bike with the black wicker basket
standing ready for the last autumn ride.

Jilted

Each time we set the clocks back
the delight of one night's
extra hour
wanes quickly the next day
when light goes out at five.

How supplely the soul slips
into North's oblique hibernation
where denuded maples
grope wanting limbs at ochre skies,

bent on being filled
with whatever luminous favour
falls prematurely westward
onto distant, more desirable
leafy boughs.

Winter Jitters

A west coast happiness
is more sublime perhaps, more intense
on account of mornings like these,
when for a few hours
the grey ethereal shutters withdraw
their dampening stupor

and if you're awake and well,
let you watch sun like glory pouring down
stretching passersby into monstrous shadows,
uncovering veins of gold in chestnut trees
and filling black capped chickadees
with winter feeding jitters
when lawn dew glitters
like baby down.

Flying in a Prop Jet in December

In the air over Michigan's woods mottled by pale snow, on the way home to Mom and Dad for the obligatory Christmas visit, news broadcasts of air crashes flash to mind—shredded metal, scattered luggage, onlookers who arrive first upon hearing the impact, rescuers in yellow rain coats (who did they come for?) I do not fear death so much as the impact, should it happen, and who would get my baseball cards, who would get my remains, and what they would have to say to what I left them. I look at the book in my hands, *Sacred Journey*, and imagine the TV picture of it lying cliché-like in the snow among the wreckage in the trees.

Waiting

The maple waits
for a warm tug
from a southern gale
that will jolt the memory
of lost youth
and burst open buds,
green eyes
lying heavy-lidded
between waking and sleep.

Vine Maple Black Ground

What draws me there
at the rounding of the schoolyard
to a fresh strand of upturned ground
at the turning of fall?
A vine maple in lace undressing,
cuddling a stretch of black earth?

It wraps gentle fingers
around an old, odd grief:
an upheaval of wanting
at once to burrow and fly.

What hands are these of mine
that lift and long to sift
and gouge black ground
to find grief's home
and lay it down?

This Pain

There's this pain
that pulses when the rain
punches the scents out of their
suffocating summer dulledness,
rising remembered
from the earth's dank ache to me.
It throbs on the back side
of a late August twilight
on the front of a fogged September dawn,
leaves but cleaves, needs.

I felt it when I stood
on the flat asphalted-over batter's box,
(what for?) where twenty years ago my feet
fit perfect in the years worn
places at home, but there's
this thin strip
of wild flowers
and lie-me-down home grass left
between the right field fence and pervading paving.
I felt it when
my weeks-old city-battered self
looked out and there's
the mountain still strong
across the still, deep bay.

This thing came
aching back when my friends
echoed their vowed I will,
and it was very good,
this world-long longed for covenant,
a willed-belonging longing,
their hands together in the pastor's grip

pulling me up short,
this pain,
and it is very good.

2

Perils

Inheritances

We carry about in us
these odd tumours of time,
of nether selves, of fathers singing distantly
and brow-furrowed mothers pealing laden
with child across fields, cityscapes,
or over seas.

Over supper table, Dad's heart
was in our stomachs, or on better days,
in that delicate silver around your neck,
when all you needed was a gentle hand
around your fears,

fears and defects rooted
in the tissue of ancestry, growing
over generations: in the subtle turn of a head,
downcast eyes, the twitch of a toe or pained
laughter at a brother stepping too close.

Congenital tumours
throb with the drum of heavy fingers
on an empty table, loaded words
and time-bred silence; they do not die
with parents or years,

only wither
in a Light, now nearly too pallid, beyond
time's contagion, that could show us
another way, a line to follow
other than blood, birth and resignation.

Grandma's Birthday

a light glows more faintly
this year in the double whorls
of Grandma's brown eyes

fastened blankly on the little boy
as she fumbles backward inside
for familiarity—the face a place

she could name and hold
as her now clawed hands cannot
nor can her worn limp legs

crawl to it if only they could
start over again
take in the clear scope

of the world like this little boy
embrace it with strong arms again
where she ran rampant once

like this little boy over unfurrowed fields
but she is lost behind brown windows
and from her home the boy recoils

and cries afraid of her murky eyes
those pools rippled with time
where he must one day lose himself

We Didn't Know

I liked the summers
when I was young in the sun
when we didn't know
that it is wrong to be idle
and go off without a plan
half-naked or all the way all day.
We didn't know
you should stay in your own yard,
that you shouldn't scavenge
other people's bottles and bicycle tires,
that the dog belongs on a leash.

But now we know:
fences are best,
spiders should be killed,
and you should sweat and dread the summer
while daylight squeezes out an extra hour,
until the mind's drained and spirit tamed.

Turning in

Anomalous west coast snows
have fallen over night and patio fixtures,
rising abominable
over fading memories of garden parties,
loping over eaves, a curling
of billowed duvets;

as if in response
the calendar slackens before turning,
heavy with this sudden call
to new year, a curved hanging on
to the old, a year delayed
by this act of God and
this curling under duvets:

white fears, cars, walks and streets.
So we turn in on ourselves
and all contained
within these plaster shells of home
under the weight
of God's growing down of grace,
for those we have
who have only us.

Break-in

she comes home and finds
her roommates looking
dazed across a scattered floor,
she all energy from play rehearsal
and they with the bad news in their eyes,
the littered floor, the open door,
and a turn of the head reveals:
computer gone, CD's, backpacks,
the violation jolting her heart
to her head,

the police, they say, have been
and gone, clueless to
who or how, but
her window's wide open, and
below there are two holes where
a ladder had pegged the dirt,
and the visions play with her—
the window,
his (her?) dirty feet,
she feels them at night
going over her bed
and out the sliding glass door
taking with them
her naiveté, so

she knows everything now
as she has not known it,
and she sees things
when she steps out:
a turn of a face,
running shoes tapping east,
the make of car on the corner,

a Kokanee bottle curb-side,
one shade drawn—all there,
seen fresh with new eyes

A Bit o' Tinsel

this Christmas the annual carols
ring while I'm in the happy maul
of the dental hygienist all in white

all is calm all is bright

she reclines me slowly
her chisel poised high
an angelic smile hanging moon-like

from the horns of her 'fifties glasses,
with at least ten other instruments
of torture splayed kinkily

on a shiny tray (oh deca-dent)
she whines reassurances
through the gaps in her teeth

so tender and mild

there, that's good, up
just a little more, good
you comfy? now

she flicks on the overhead T.V.
where the Price Is Right
lies embedded in the ceiling tiles
my favorite show, she peals

sleep in heavenly peace

there above in Christmas trim
appears the loot—electric range, a full

fridge, an orange deco love seat, and

a year's supply of doggie chow—my mouth
drooling as the novocaine sinks in now
she dickers with Doctor over the right price

at least another 400, 500 dollars,
I'm thinking, before this feeling's gone
whir and grind, whir grind grind

jingle bells, jingle bells

powdered teeth showering everywhere
(a white Christmas for Doctor)
then the bit snags on dentine, whoops

huh? I say, but he's already asking
about my job, what I do, forgetting
that metal whirring between my jaws

o'er the fields we go

I search for the easiest way to say
"unemployed"—but "nussing" is all
that gurgles out, What's that?

he really wants to know, I just sweat
and manage a faint cry
as he packs the holes with everlasting tinsel

Pacific Farming

Between the house and cow yard,
wearing holes in a knit sweater,
he's making a go of it
in the Pacific mud sucking
at his gum boots. He picks
at the cow dung under his nails,
looks across the Holstein herd,
and sees through the rain the outline
of his little girl in the high pasture
going flat out toward the sea. She likes

the squeak of her boots on the grass,
the rain patting her olive green rain coat
and the way the cows tear the grass,
and she knows nor wants no other. He

contemplates the stock,
biting his lip—high bony
buttocks carrying udders
thick-veined with white gold—
and he knows
mastitis could turn
the whole herd for the worse.
He shivers as his little girl,

hid in the herd, reaches up one hand
and swats a knobby rump. Her "Come boss!"
rips the misty sheet, and with a bellow
the liquid gold turns home.

The Teller

I took two English courses,
one guy wanted ideas,
the other one wanted commas and colons,
so I failed 'cause
I wrote commas for the wrong guy.
Then I took math,
you know that section—imaginary numbers?
I said what the hell is this? If they
don't exist why am I learning it, if it's not here
what good is it, you know what I mean?
If it's not gonna make my life better
forget it.
Gimme hard solid facts,
something that's not gonna change
every time I look at it.
Like 2.
A 2 is a 2 is a 2.
You wake up tomorrow, 2
is still gonna be 2.

Unless you're married of course,
then you can't be sure. I was married.
Once I woke up, she was gone. Two kids,
she took 'em both, don't know where.
Been five years, no, five and three months.
Trevor, he called me Da. Melissa loved lady bugs,
kept 'em in her piggy bank, flying pennies
she said, plink plink against porcelain,
whirligigs make baby pennies. Screw! Screw!
Don't know where she learned that.

I work at a bank now, solid job,
two plus two make four every day, you know.

And I still get them Christmas presents
every December, even if they are only
imaginary numbers.

Divining on the Beach

under the trees on blankets
a huddle of women
watch the food
their men and children playing nearby

a Chinese family of mostly girls
stretches in the sun
and one big white guy
fondles pensively the long hair of one

through the air
hurtle fluorescent toys
spheres ellipses and rings
acting and reacting
planets in a plastic universe

cycles crisscross
and joggers' bottoms jiggle
along the beach path

one little boy shovels up sand
trying to contain the shore in a pail
and carry it home

a blond girl
bulging from her bikini
into the sand
slaps the boy lying beside her
for touching
reaching for a piece of
what isn't his

cargo ships lumber

out in the deep
having found what they came for

while on the dock oriental voices
inflect ritual tones
divining with hooked lines on poles
over the sea
for its slippery silver
the air rank with the smell

swaggering up the beach
is a white-bearded man
wagging a stick
like Moses in blue jeans
except that the waters do not part
and no one is following
he not having found
his power or his people

Electric Joy

Interrupting my afternoon nap
under cherry blossoms in the park,
he comes humming
in his state of the art high voltage wheel chair,
buzzing, jogging
over ruts and holes, eye balls
lolly-bobbing toward me,
        I think: taxes, medicare. Am I
        paying for chariots now?
cigarette wagging
like a maestro's baton unlit from his mouth.
He crooks his fingers around his joy stick
and crunches a wake through the gravel path,
eyeing me.
        What is it? A light? My time?
        My talk? I poise for the transaction.
Then he stops, buzzes back, forward,
two turns left and right, and a pirouette
choreographing whorls in loose stone
like a Buddhist temple garden, pulls aside
and cocks his head to the freshly sculped ground.

Leaning into a trash can,
he grunts his muse to the paper brew,
drools a line that hangs and quivers.
He stirs, and pulls out a well-done pizza box
and holds it to his lighter,
raises it *flambé* to the cherry blossoms
waffling down. Contemplation.
        Somebody help him. I rise
as he turns on his electric joy,
carves a few more loops in stone,
wild loose screws,

waxing lyrical to the sky,
old pizza sparks in a petaled wind.
Then he looks me rye in the eye
with a crazed grin, and taps a crooked exit
with a finger to his head.

Swimming By Zen

At the YMCA, Mrs. Dalai Lama, our lifeguard coos:
swimming is meditation,

after one lap, I pull up coughing
sucking when I should have blown

just let the whole body relax, you're trying too hard,
the breathing, breathe to your rhythm

left goggle lens fills with water
and the suction on the right
won't let go

let yourself go, become part of the water

oh God, only seven laps,
body feels like a bronze Buddha,
curse the family name,
a long line of lard asses

flutter kick like this, she shows me
on the deck in T-shirt and shorts
especially people with heavy bottoms

tracing the black line six feet under
through chlorinated, baby blue space

cup the hands just a little like this

nine-and-a-half, toes grope
for solid ground

make an "S" with your arms, close to the body,

reach and pull
don't think too much,
feel

> barely conscious of her noise out
> there in terrestrial nether world

push yourself a little
you can do almost twenty-five,
thirty, if you want

> thirteen-and-a-half

just flow, feel the energy of the water
don't fight it

> thirteen and a half, I
> pull my Buddha bottom up
> (barely)
> onto the edge, sit,
> gaze down
> at the crease in my naval,
> listen to nothing
> but the rhythm of wheezing breath

Dalai Lama waggles over,
her karmic eyes in my face
You don't look so good,
you're not in shape, are you.

> I say nothing

Are you still with me?

> No, I'm not here, I sigh.

What are you doing, what's happening?

I'm meditating like you told me,
now get the hell out of my space

you know, I think you eat too much,
only eat just enough, no more

thank you, I smile
I think I got it now:
this is Nirvana
and I am nothing.

Lost Souls

On a late afternoon stroll,
squinting into an unsettling haze,

the trickery of sun setting masqueraded
a solitary figure, though familiar,

materializing slowly before me. He cast
a deep-throated hello and an incantation

(or an invitation?) to join him
at the Lost Souls celebration among the trees

in the park on All Hallows Eve. A smile
of recognition quivered between us,

then revived and reconstituted, with
a gleam in his eye, he glided on.

A Vancouver Rain in June

A boy is caught squinty-eyed,
and a woman in T-shirt and shorts,
clutching her bare arms, teeth clenched
against the bite of the rain.

A school girl passes with her studded denim jacket
draped as a suitable sacrifice overhead,
while a man stands trapped
with only half his hair under the eaves,
unable to cross the street.
He glances up in search of the last drop
in a long freight train of rain passing by.

Beneath a sidewalk café parasol
sits another woman, oblivious,
with a novel and cappuccino,
who has learned the discipline
of a Vancouver rain in June.

Lily Xu's Tailor Shop

Vancouver girl
speaks of Taipei New Years,
vendors, and Chinese markets,
of foods with foreign names
and antique art,

of an absent father back home
cheating on Mom
and a suicidal uncle
who watches grandfather all day
ramble on about how it was

and still must be
back there in Shanghai:
friends and streets
she will know no more
as they were then

as they were then
in multi-coloured detail
(sometimes black and white)
that only her memory
mends as it weaves.

On My Name for Mrs. Xu*

My friend's mom can't say my name
no matter how much we shape
her tongue and mouth
around the awful sounds—

Two syllables, Mom, say it: Ka-rl.

But for Mrs. Xu it all crawls out so
torturously, ponderously slow
as Carol, Kalo, Kawo,
Kar or Ka.

Never mind, I try to reassure,
just call me Dick.

*Xu, pronounced "shoe"

West Broadway

mama pushing the stroller
baby hangs over
staring down the dog
of the drunk weaving
along West Broadway
a long yarn
to the mannikins
suspended in a store front glaze
like cold lava
glassy-eyed   red dress   low black heels

the young teen girl
in bus number nine pulling away
wants the shoes

all sizes clicking by
around beast and babe
lemon carts   news   asparagus
while great white sparks
arc down trolly rain
from a heaven
wired for motion
and no time
for high school girls' contemplation

50% Off Mummy

Outside "please mum" boutique
behind a rack of jump suits
and little dresses 50% off
hides a mum,
                    all except for
her dark eyes
peering over
under brown smooth hair,

and two ratty knees in blue jeans
and sandaled feet
below,
minus bust and torso.

He waits from his perch
on a coffee shop stool
                    for mum to step out
from little girls' jump suits
and pull herself together,
to give him the full view:

the length of her hair,
the shape of her breasts, waist, hips,
how delicate the fingers
that play a bar of plastic hangers,
how thin or thick mum's lips
and what they would tell
if she were whole.

Looking Back

Summer bound by
brush flanked creeks
nostalgic with thongs and toes,
with sun
flashing in pop can lids
and two tuna sandwiches on a beech towel,

regrets fall back
sad and innocent onto grassy knolls—
the black flow of her hair over
budding breasts, promises she held
for unknown beds and beaus—regrets
that have ripened with a season of men.

Rules of Chess

1. The king is your chief end, the other pieces minor players in the game, luring and eluding under your hand.

2. Your pawn moves only forward, ignorant to your plan, waiting for your call, left often and forgotten in the extremities of your view. Your voice comes to the pawn only softly and strange, at last, in your moment of need.

3. And your hand moves like a ghost, your voice a distant nibble on the plastic membrane. But I need you up close, to hear you over the table again: pasta and red wine, your hand feathered in mine over the landscape of our common need.

4. So if you move me for a cause other than us, your master plan at hand, please forfeit this game and move on to another one.

Standing Naked

Standing naked by the bath tub
when the phone rings, wet,
he cradles the handle
of a fragile conversation —

        the girl at the party,

yes I remember,

        just wanted to say hi, she says,

uhuh —

he blushes, her voice there
uncovering him,
he remembers the chit-chat games
from the night before,
the loaded gestures, intentions, regrets,
now dripping like a reluctant rain
and echoing off the tiled walls,
shrinking in on him.
He hangs
on her words, his words,
groping for a towel, for something he's lost,
the phone cord stretching
like an umbilical cord
beyond him through a crack in the door.

Damp Sheet

it was just a phrase,
the tailing of a conversation,
that hung regrettable between them
like a damp sheet

collecting the dust
of unspoken feelings,
leaving him stuttering apologies,
sudden gusts

blowing warm airs on wet words—
the sheet flicks up,
billows, falls—
trying to fill the dead air,

but it's still there, just a phrase,
hanging damp like a sheet
that has numbed two lovers dumb

Wobbly Legs

This table of roughly hewn boards
rests on wobbly legs, but
how can we know the risk
when we feel no fear or doubt?

How can we take the chance
of me forgiving you,
you forgiving me, if sin
and imperfection do not exist,
making us quiver each time
we put our cups out on the table?
How can we take the chance
if I *just forget about it*:

how you left the dinner table
without a word,
the last bite of apple cobbler
stuck in my throat? when we
do not even know the sadness
of these bitter morsels falling
from our unsteady table of *que sera*?

Drinking Alone

I walk the street
brewing a discontented hour,
no other flesh and bone
to draw from this mix
I'm filled to the full with,
and when I've done with
I'll take in more. Rain
misting toward me
through the vapour lamp
wets my throat,
seals this T-shirt
close to my chest.

Shades

Nigel's off to stay with family;
Jason's in Mexico; Ian and family
in the Valley, Sandra gone back home
to Germany, and the fondness for me
in Hans' eyes while
I waved from the sidewalk
in jockey shorts and short brown socks,

casting shades in empty places.

I do not eat, just wait
by the phone for
someone turning back perhaps,
perhaps some benign news,
and watch T.V.
where announcers babble bland clichés
and men in uniforms
swing with sticks
at stitched white balls
and run from home
going home:
going, going, gone.

Were We to Go

Were we to go on public opinion
on families' plans and well-meaning friends,
playing it safe and predictable, you and I,
apart,

never confronting the puzzle
between us, tumbling in the right combinations
of skin colour and creed (click!)
of age and the right amount of greed,

knowing who to date,
how far to go
when these carnal urges stir,
when not to hold hands, kiss,

without risk of pain or ambiguity,
with everyone on our side,
at our sides,
without the 'you and I'.

Portable Zenith LCD
(for Nathan)

What do I say when they ask
what I do,
each day, for work?
I get up,
I bask in the glow
of liquid
crystal
display,
this play glow, this crystal, so liquid
when glowing in crystal display,
I play in it, I fidget,
curse and mumble incantations,
caressing with finger tips the plastic globes
until the liquid washing before my eyes
crystallizes
with a luster
somewhat recognizable.

Bites for Kids

Saw the president on the tube,
and Gore,
at a school in Modesto California,
running wires through walls to make
a highway through cyberspace
for kids,
for votes,
doling out the lines—

"so America's children can
interact (without action) and
interface (without facing)
on the information highway."

And I can already see
the tiny info bites
crunching, lip-smacking down the line
for Mackinaw Michigan,
coming out Alpha-Bits in the classroom
at the other end.

Feeding Amoebas

What is this that
makes you want to watch missiles on CNN
through the computer screens of U.S. navy planes?

makes you want to see them come
through the cross hairs—tomahawks, cruise
and sidewinders—accelerate and
zero in on concrete blocks sitting
like Saddam Husein's toys, grey and still?

Watch them worlds away,
watch the silent bombs (military intelligence
says they're smart) homing in in your
living room. Impact: zap and white-out,
feeding morbid curiosity like dill cream cheese
on honey bagels on a Sunday afternoon.
Feed your ravenous amoeba,

watch him ebb and flow and twist
to the shapes of Muslim mosques,
around mothers on the road to visit a friend,
around the laugh of boys running broken streets
or the dying from want of food and care,
to the shapes of fathers looking for bread
or a safe place
to bathe, or pray.

We Should Feel Good

President Bush said
we should feel good about it:
twenty missiles hit their targets
and only three went astray
that killed eight...
"collateral" I think he said,
like a promissory note
with a pledge to return.

Disgruntled

Don't be, the boss says.
    I don't want to be, I say.
And he, I don't want you to be.
    But I am! I say, I am
    only human
    with feelings,
    like angry right now, like any
    when his hard-won cash
    is held back
    close-fistedly.
    I am only asking
    for a little fairness.
The boss swivels and stares.

Mary later tells me, Life isn't fair.
    You croon the creed
    of the avaricious, I say.
The code of humanity, she says,
you can't expect him to care.
    Jesus Christ! I say, don't *you* care!
Jesus Christ? she says, I'm only human too.

Dead in the Water

Talking with the boss is not
like reading the book
with the spinnaker port side
and main sail starboard,
two pages full
pulling together
many strands, many knots.

Dead in the water
is within arm's length of the boss
in an opposing cushioned chair
where the brains sit
speaking of vacancies   layoffs,
                                        a vision
                                                    and regrets,
telling of unfortunate oversights while I
see nothing but an endless sea flat beyond me
and he not noticing, hearing a thing I say,
not even the draft
or whistle through the ears.

Hymns from the Basement

Bent over, there he spins
on the grass,
totaling last night's waste:
beer cans, a case, substances
in liquid, dust and skin thin paper,
waffling still somewhere
where he cannot trace what he had
or attach himself to it,
cannot gain gravity
propelled by an indistinguishable force
out of orbit.

His stereo beats from the basement,
his hymns—
thump,
thump thump,
thump,
thump thump—
the devil's pulse
just under the skin, my floor,
vibrating leg-wise to my core,
connecting him to me;
I try to lift my feet
to break his hold,
but the bastard's got me
sure as gravity.

He comes to the door
for a roll of TP—even
a couple squares to spare?
so drunk
I wonder why he cares.

He's at the door again,
this time a sunken figure,
reddened eyes,
head hanging by a thread,
waiting to present his offering.
What now? An untimely greeting?
a beer? food he has no use for?
He is already mouthing his placation,
thick malted words as empty as a bottle,
waiting to suck me out and in.

When rodents
come out in the dark:
they nibble at your ears,
teasing at first,
finally chewing
until your ears are raw;
they suck
the sweet sleep from your head,
squeaking in and out of orifices
like Swiss cheese
until you lose your head and
you are gone
mad.

I'm turning inside,
him downstairs
in there, raising hell again.
I think
thoughts I've never thought,
even how to do it—
bat? hammer? gun? (if I had one)
several brief steps down
and snuff out hell.
And I pray,

I pray I don't
turn upside down.

Ben

Somebody told me once,
truth is in your head,
only what you make it.

A distant friend called me the other day,
said,
"Teresa's dead,
killed," and
that you did it Ben,
that you're in jail.

That's all.
The words stuck terse,
like a knife in my gut,
sudden as breath.

I heard you laugh together,
laughed with you,
the three of us
foraging through garage sales
on Saturday afternoon,
saw you into your new home
with warm accolades,
hoped with you for a child,
long nights over lattes. I
even have your end table still
decked with a potted spider plant.

What did I miss? Something
in the sum of your exchanges,
a turn of her head
that disparaged you?
or a despairing tremble

below your grateful tones,
a twitch in the heavy fingers
that lifted your cup?

My friend, speak,
please say they're wrong,
that what I'm hearing
is all in my head, or yours.

Retards

Some say that a mom's emotional state
during the time she's pregnant with you
can effect your development.
I don't know if I believe it, but sometimes I wonder
what she was thinking while she had me, and
how the fact that my sister was born mentally retarded,
two years before me, affected my retardation.

Our Back Alley

I remember the way
the grass crept up tufted
through the pebble-pocked alley,
school kids' shoes and bike tires
pressing the fragile blades down again
in the cyclic game of advance and retreat,
and the way you looked down to round
the potholes, how imperfect, yet
every stone in its appointed place.

Now I look out,
and the pavement is still smoking
where the city crew invaded,
scorching the lane to a sheen,
with a clean edge of black ash against lawn,
the way a quick blade
glints and slits soft flesh.

The Hazing

It's in the alley of our block
where Neighbors gather for the hazing
on beach chairs, in sunglasses and shorts
knocking back beers: our lawn the stage,
our Cherry Tree the lead. A chain saw sings
from the thick forearm of a stubble-cheeked lad,
the Thug hired for a cameo. And there
the main Antagonist stands, hands on hips
on the other side of the fence, barking up
at the branches he wants *off!*
the ones reaching over to his side.
Neighbours approve or jeer the actors
like the original Shakespeare audience:
That one there,
Just give it one cut
take it off,
This one's got to come down,
right here, that's all.
we can take her this way
no, that one.
No, that's too much!
if we tie her up here
Yeah, take that off too!
It's lopsided now.
and a pulley there.
Don't leave that
It's not your fucking tree
sticking up
Another cut on this side
by itself
I have to live with it
like a phallus.
right in the crotch.

the rest of my life.

It won't scar too bad

Now who's going

if we just leave enough.

to pick up the pieces?

That's enough!

I'm outa here.

There, that might do.

Enough. Enough. Enough.

A Conversation

It wasn't till mid-August
I noticed one slender tendril of vine
had fingered through the fence
from my side to his, to the guy
who'd never talk to me again,
and there my finest squash
lay filling out on his side,
irretrievable, I let it lie.

It grew for days,
an unintended unattended grace
like the finger of God,
my squash's conciliatory stretch,

until a September afternoon
with the back door closing on summer,
the squash appeared in its prime

without a word
on my side,
unattached and alone on the lawn,
as he willed it.

No Room Under the Christmas Tree

Get the manger scene outa there! one of them said,
as the presents come flinging out
from many hands at the foot of the Christmas tree
knocking over two wise men and a shepherd.
The room was rife with the sights and sounds of bacchanalia,
bleary-eyed kids, the stretch marks of holiday malls
on Mom and Dad, sweaty palms and migraines,
all pulled taut in red and green and lace and fake
snow flakes across the windows and walls. The scene

was a feeding frenzy, a feast of ripping and gouging
(all the lovely Christmas paper) and a gorging with
the wonderful insides, some morsels pushed aside.
The pillage ended, exhausted and bloated, they waded
through the flood and debris of boxes and bows,
and under the tree the rest of the wise men and shepherds lay
out cold, Mary and Joseph too, too much to handle in one day,
except for baby Jesus who was still smiling up from his wooden
crib, and in the calm of aftermath I think I heard him giggle.

3

Promise

Rumours

A scandal's abroad God
took flesh and bone,
crammed the divine into time
and ate dry bread, cried
and bled when a chisel slipped
in his father's shop, where he
first saw his end in his hand,
bloodying the splintered earth

and the devout blush,

the face of God
sitting pimpled
behind a school desk,
squinting to make out
the word of God;

outside in the evening light
a young woman passing casts
a glance God's way,
slender arms embracing a pitcher
on the path to the well, tapping
a warm rush though God's blood,

making the devout blush.

The word is, God
plodded through mud,
got athlete's foot
and jock itch, sweat and stank
and fell exhausted
(too much walking
for God in one day) and

falling asleep in the rain,
he dreamed:
        his feet sucking down
        in wet earth,
        leper's hands reaching,
        prostitutes on a side street,
        the devout jeering,
and bolting awake, he shook
and tried to keep his sanity
till dawn broke his daily bread.

The Blooding

Under the echo
of a hollow salutation
an old voice stops me
in the stairwell,

and crusts obtrude—old talk,
expired commitments,
dead grievances—layered
in my memory
like scabs,

sores of another day
oozing in the clammy grip
of his hand in mine: time's
distilling squeeze
let it bleed one last time
(let it bleed).

Chehalis: Christmas Eve 1996

Full moon rises
like The Baptist—
from the wood-thronged river
to wash maples snow-clad—
afoot on clouds;

the radiant wood
a pageant in still frame
waits, strains east
this eve over the river
for the cry from Bethlehem.

Chehalis Christmas

The sun swings shallow
through solstice, glancing subtle
across peaks purple-veined
beneath snowdust,
a blue stillness in the heart;

a baby coos
from the river-ripped valley
amid an avalanche of song
tongued up by candle flame
and rum and eggnog
on his day, laughter of a baby

winging on eagles
down the Chehalis river course,
life in its breath, to the listless
who hug the banks, and hope:
still blue mountain
quake of snowdust down.

Thaw

A huddle of girls in a damp thaw
of after-school sun: on the road, one is
head down leaning home, the young one

hands under the arms of her wool coat,
and the middle one skipping backward,
all giddy as a heat wave in April town.

Lap it up, sisters, undulate and sing,
blaze as one new born child
over snow-patched, potholed streets.

Visit With a Heavenly Host

On the roof of Barry's home
while the rest sleep below
he and I play guests with a twelve-inch scope
to the host of heaven awhile—
he stretches out the heavens like a tent

That's Circle Nebula, Barry says,
there.

A circle? I say.
Cool, like eternity.
he brings out the starry host
and calls them each by name
So I take a look, but Circle's just a ghostly mass.

They call it M57 too, he says.

Oh, more like a steak sauce, I guess.

Here, he points, Jupiter's moons.

Hmm, a bit jiggly in this glass,
but okay, I do see five or maybe six.

There's only two or three actually,
and Saturn's rings, see?

Not like the picture in my grade four
science book, but yes they're there, I agree.

That galaxy straight up, over
two hundred million stars.

I crane my neck. My God!
who is man that you are mindful of him?

See there on the horizon coming up,
a red star about to explode, Beetle Juice.

That should be interesting, I muse.

No it won't, he says, it'll be as bright as the sun.

So, double the fun, we need more sun.

Devastating, you see,
one sun this bright is just right.

the stars of the heavens will dissolve
and the sky be rolled up like a scroll

And there is Orion,
it has special memories for me,
good and bad.

What's the good?

I proposed to Fiona
when Orion appeared through the clouds.

And the bad?

Some other night,
no, not tonight.

Promises

Eight planets on a line,
they promised us on the news,
just above the southern horizon,
the last such alignment for ninety-five years.
Watch it while you can's the word,

as stock markets wobble,
astrologers juggle sums and constellations,
and apocalypse looms for some,

I wait at the fringes
of earth's evening gown
back lit in purple pastel
like some religious fanatic
waiting for the second coming,
expecting to see the mobile solar system
I made of wire and string and styrofoam
in elementary school: a little Mercury,
a little bigger Venus, red Mars,
an orange and very large Jupiter,
Saturn striped and ringed, Uranus (still
makes me giggle) inscrutable Neptune, and way out, Pluto,
all in a perfect line, I thought.

All minus Earth, they said. Then,
not eight but just two bright,
unidentifiable lights appear
like an abbreviated kite tail hanging
from a billowing moon.

My binoculars hang, betrayed, and
I turn back to my world out of line,
thinking perhaps my grandkids will return

in another ninety-five years
after their mobile planets, like mine,
hang out of reach in the attic:
styrofoam promises all jumbled in a box
waiting to be aligned.

Vancouver's Annual Fireworks Display: 10:15 PM, August 18, 1993

Fire speaks to fire, like eyes
alive in the night, the music
whiffing across the bay.
Sea urchins fling skyward
tingling phosphorescently,
lines of colored fire
criss-crossing in perfect 4/4 time.
Ooo! there goes Tina Turner's hair,
rockets wiggle up sperm-like
and explode, shimmering, ahhh!
blasts that shake the black night.

Then,
no one came for it,
waited or watched for it,
but someone answers back,
above the fireworks display,
when unscheduled lights appear,
singly, brief, burning white then out,
arcing across the scene
from somewhere in the dark beyond.
Some witnessed them — one,
two, three...
I saw four falling
out of synchronism with the music below.

Stilted Landscape
June 21, 8:35 PM

solstice bends sprinklers
in the park
to mobile rainbows

in red yellow orange
six dancers on stilts
ribbon maypoles

around home base
aluminum bats ting
pop flies to the outfield

where mother
and a child call
their cocker spaniel

dogging foul balls
through stilts
ribbons and rainbows
in a solstice mist

No Grace Meal

An abundant offering
of March *manna* falls
all day on Kitsilano
before the Sabbath rest,

and the ungracious ground
gathers it in too quickly,
dissolving and sucking up
the white hosts whole, swallows

all the while overlooking
the customary thanks,
without pause for reflection
or a perfunctory amen

for these miracle morsels
dropping endless down
in glittering relief
from a tireless giver.

Between Season

Good-bye forever, once again,
to soaked marine socks
raincoated beaches and dogs
shaking in their tracks
cold moist fur,
indoor's dark dreams
of when the rain would end or
how to end it all
evaporating
(thank God)

as we squeegee water spots
from the west window,
the fields behind us
trying to dry,

good-bye forever we say
as the rusted end of a spade
slips wistful into soil,
nudging the neighbour's fence,
and back doors crack
open a vein of gold
in the western sky.

Fish Bone Sky

At the beach
we consider clouds:
the sky all fish
scales of gray white
and bones playing the blue
crests of waves
that riddle and wake,
break and whittle away.
Our toes ply sand,
think of flying with fish,
think of stranding our selves
there across the blue July.

On an Octopus in Okisollo

1.

From the hour we arrive,
pitching camp in the dark
at the landing north of Campbell River,
rain pours all night,
and the next day, patter patter
on the paddle into Okisollo Channel.
We shiver, hunched
over our lunches on no-name beach,
wondering out through the mist
where our friends must be,
and contemplate abandoning
the five-day voyage
and Octopus Island
for Owen Bay and ice cream.

2.

First contact:
bows slide up on brown algae
and sandals scuff barnacled rock.
First thought: turn back
from this holy virgin land;

        but with one step the next is easy:
we claim plots for tents, one foot-fall
snaps saplings easily to form bed mats,

        branches removed from ordained landings
light quickly and become camp smoke

trailing up to night hawks
gliding the dusk with clean *peents!* calling
to our laughter and mingling
incongruous through an ocher night.

3.

I am a foreigner here,
I must remember, not my own boss,
going by another's rules and for the life of me
must obey the currents and skies,
and hoping for my mates' sakes
that they are too. And in this
three-fold agreement,
I, my fellows and the Ruler of this place,
we find a rhythm
of companionship and grace.

4.

The flood tide has pitched us
on this Octopus Island,
three tents staking our claim
with the clatter of camp pans,
hiss of a stove, ruffling
of a tarp in a waft of wind
in isolated companionship;

and we already anticipate the next wave
that will wash us seaward,
seeking other havens, more
mossy rocks perhaps and sun,
more places to set up

our curiosity shops
for sharks, snakes and fawn.

5.

The west-bent sun
mottles clouds a dusky red
and a hand stretching in off the horizon
caresses the channel
to a sheet of frosted glass;
then from a strand of rocks across the water,
through the cries of gulls,
somebody with bagpipes bellows
moanful tones: another poet traveler
looking for a home.

6.

Just when we think
we have the place figured out,
a maple leaf, perfectly formed,
comes floating up to the edge
below our toes on the rocks,
though we look about and find
only fir and pine.

7.

An eagle plunges to the bay,
talons stretch, penetrate,
and reversing

in pendulum harmony
she rises
on slow motion power,

as two gulls screech up
after the catch
reaching for a handout:

the have and the have-not's
just like back home, I think,
on my little stretch of West Broadway.

8.

Out here objectivity decays:
clouds become lightly cooked broccoli
        or a man in fez,
arbutus trees become nut brown women
        washing clothes at the shore,
beach boulders your fallen guards
        faithful to the death;
gulls are amused onlookers
and the mountain a bushy elephant
        with one beady eye on the bay.

Waves, they are no longer reactions
        to the action of wind
but wrestlers,
        conniving a way to turn a kayak
        with one deft reversal,
and wind is the firm hand of your father
        guiding you home, where exhausted
you loosen your hold
with brine the saliva of a tossing dragon

spattered on your forearm.

9.

This delicate island of fern and fawn
and crusty pines, wedging a hold,
coming stunted under ocean squalls,

roots blending congenially to the contours
of worm and stone, together tilling
and shaping, all tended undeterred

through the ages by the hand of God
though a stranger's heel may slip, dislodging
a cushion of moss whose life has clung

for years above the surf, and
the stranger's heart sinks and stirs
as the ungracious guest, where

the forever forgiving gardener
has stood watch over many such ruptures
ready to heal and amend.

10.

When our kayaks slip from the shore for home
before sunrise on the last morning,
and our bows break the subtle ruffles
of frosted glass, we think naively
that we have left nothing more than tracks
and our shit in the woods. But as I

pivot for one last time-stopping glance,
above the rocks on the shore stands a buck
knee deep in salal, ripping leaves from a tree,
then pausing for a minute, he and I, eye to eye,
amaze over who is watching who: two fragile creatures,
irresistibly, irreversibly changed in the parting.

100 Grams of Armenian Brandy

A cancelled play draws us back
to her mother's flat,
a minimalist set but for
the gaudy, garage-sale prints,
flowers in flimsy lacquered frames,
a place where I find the history
of the girl's lucid smile;
daughter, mother, the unplanned guest,
the way they've always liked it,
I guess, back home:

her mother
ties up a loose coil of hair
revealing the same supple neck
and pulls out her last 100 grams
of Armenian brandy (just enough
to color the air) saved for
this guest she's never met;
100 grams of Armenian history
spill into the patio sky,

a mix of rolled and guttural "r's"
in unabated Armenian English
ruffling like leaves of a fresh book:
        five years of post-*perestroika*
        bringing twenty dollars a month
        with inflated prices, books and
        jewelry selling for food; candles
        burning only one hour of night throwing
        family and friends back on each other
        reciting favourite books once owned,
and laughter

as we are now,
mother, daughter, unplanned guest,
while the air is still burning with
one brief hour of Armenian brandy.

Valentine's Eve in Vancouver

She's German, he American,
dining on Valentine's Eve,
the bombing of Dresden fifty years past,
his uncle perhaps a pilot that day,
and her father the next walked
the shell torn streets
among skeletal ruins that once
held the pulse of the city's innocents;

they are as children, oblivious to Dresden,
and concern themselves instead
with the clutter and chatter of this day:
an assignment due, exams,
a dictatorial boss he'd like to eliminate
and the particularities of Indian food,
how it warms comfortably in the stomach.
And lifting two glasses in an Indian café on Granville
they smile and drink to Valentine's Day.

Peeling Oranges

You peel away the skin of that orange
like the first time we really talked
on the beach front bench,
where you unraveled
with each word pressed just so
like finger tips:
pungent cells of citrus
bursting
a thousand worlds
about us.

To Know

your smile
undressing you
undresses me
when we lie

a lifetime

two life lines
uttered from our lips
seeking a merger of

purpose

in eyes
unfolding a joining
deeper than sex

breath

convecting
the air around us
God's imparting

companionship

we wait
face to face
and seek the gift

to know

A Light Alarm

The perennial apple
of our enterprise rises;
light waking through
cherry limbs and rusty rails,
curls over patio leaves;

the veins pulse with sense
and responsibilities,
faith in possession pressing
on bus and boss
under the day's hastening arch,

while from our deck dappled
in labour's first light
muffled amens are whispered
of work unseen, unheard, in
the mauve wink of a leaf's edge.

Sisyphus and Grace

There are times Sisyphus is right:
when I'm hired two times in one year
and laid off three,
or the day I got my tax rebate
and paid my car insurance the next,
or when I fixed the carburetor,
started the car and sprang a water leak,

when the rock rolls back over me.

But there are times when grace has a day,
like finding that '54 Ford transmission
when I needed it in the twelve-car junk yard in Arizona,
or that guy on his golf cart at hole thirteen
stopping by with a cup of ice water,
or when I was laid off one day
and my boss was fired the next.

Bargaining Committee

The night before day one of labour union negotiations
I dream: my father in a hole,
crows flocking
to their balcony seats
on winter limbs, matching insults,
and father picking at the dirt
with the blunt end of an old spade,
calling me: Come on in.
        No, Dad, the rain is coming
        the crows are coming round
        and I'm in the union now.

I bolt up, his visage there at the foot of my bed.
You're in a what, Son!
        A union. You know, like... together.
They forced you in then?
        Volunteered. I... I'm
        on the bargaining committee, Dad.
You disappoint me, Son.
                                He disappears.

Day one, the opposition glares across the table
sipping lawyer's fees from porcelain cups,
I reach an ancestral hand back to my wallet
still there through denim blue jeans. Proceed.
It's all volleyball. One, two set, spike. Regroup, serve.
We break for the day, only ten or so to go
and I jitter out the door
on the fine edge of a caffeine buzz
into a cold spring sun. Squint. And I hear Dad again
sifting through the high rises, through the exhaust
and walks of the city churn.
        You getting paid for this, Son?

Getting In to Come Out

A contrary rain
foils the road on our way
to the ski slopes,
forcing us inside

where we share a kettle and
murmurs of ourselves meet
in the warmth between us,
selves we've never heard, that were
locked inside when skies were fairer,
when work had kept us out,

and inside us eddies form
as the rain hits the road,
a slow swelling down stream
that forces the honest,
the hard-working out.

Common Grace

Bathroom walls usually read
like anal cliches, like
fortunes from twisted cookies
inspired in a constipated stall. But

in the loo at the Blue Moon I look around
and there see my name in print! "Karl sucks."
And turning my head right I read,
"Did you know God loves even you?"

So I reckon now by bathroom grace:
even though I suck, God still loves me. Or
on another day, if I'm reading right to left:
though God loves me, I still suck.

In

I was a racist and a bigot one week, and sexist the next, because of a thing I wrote, a not so innocent story with some nasty nasty people in it, not our kind, not anyone you'd ever find in our fair city of love, of brother/sisterhood. So they set that story to flames and me toward the city gates. I met a black guy there sitting alone on a stone, asked him his name.

Intolerant, he said, three years.

I'm Racist, I said, just got here. Why don't you go back in?

They can't stand me there.

Me neither, hate my guts.

Whadj'all do? he said.

Made a story with a guy who talked with an accent, I said.

That's it?

No, this guy called Chinese Chinks, Mexicans Wetbacks and Blacks Spicks.

Pretty bad, man.

Yup, I said. What did you do?

Preached 'bout a perfect world, with people more like me.

Yeah, yer not bad. I could like you, be like you.

Me too, man. Then he looked at me and said, You wanna hang here with me?

I'm in, I said.

And then he reached for my hand.

Fred

I'm well
taken care of, got lots of friends:

one knows everything about computers,
mine's never so down he can't fix it,

and another one I can always call when *I'm* down,

one works out with me, pushes me hard,

another at work will always cover my ass

and one at the stock exchange tells me where to stick my cash,
a sure bet.

But Fred, Fred can't fix a thing,
totally useless:
can't get me tickets or an audition when I need it,
knows nothing about money, knows
everything about nothing, and sometimes
hardly says a thing, just sits there
and furrows his brow with incomprehension
at how I try to make him understand. He
tracks mud into my house and then leaves, so that
he's always there when I don't need him,
like a broken shovel, my useless friend
never giving me anything I need
so there's no books to balance between us:
so wonderfully free and useless.

For Prabo Mihindukulasuriya

When I was a kid I wondered
how long it would take
to dig a hole all the way
through the earth to the other side
to China or Sri Lanka, and
who I'd find when I got there.
Now I know

because he's here, and I know
digging would take too long,
just too long to find him. It takes
a miracle, like what happened
last August when the guy, he
just dropped out of the clouds
in a fat 747 with blinking lights.

For Rudy Wiebe
upon reading *A Discovery of Strangers:*

which made me see the first White's black boot
thudding the shore of Tetsot'ine land,
see the dull stubs of the Elder's teeth
chewing over implications for his child,

made me feel the steel of a barrel
and the smell of gun shot,
made me chew fermented moss
and savor smoked cariboo stomach,

which made me taste one summer in a Vancouver café
the chilly sludge of an iced mocha
drawn up through a candy-striped straw
and feel it settle with a syrupy thud
in a stomach gone slack of memory.

Broken Lines

Studies completed, this graduation leaves me with:
two ragged notebooks under a dry pen, three Coke cans,
a mug sitting on my desk collecting spores,

stories unfinished,
broken lines of verse
(on stray napkins and scraps of newspaper, on
the back of an unanswered letter by my bed)
and a drama still to play in the dark corner of my head,

Graduation must be exercised this year
while I commence with work to be done,
though the letter from the university bids me come,
asks me:
    my size of cap and gown?
    do I want a photo? how many
    tickets for my friends?
You're all invited, you'll see my full name
inside the program
and a contented gap yawning
in the line of caps and gowns (somewhere in the P's)
and hear the sound, I pray, of God clapping down.

Mongolian Grill

the party descends
on Mongolian Grill smorgasbord
bok choy   peppers   thin strips of lamb
and onions
sizzling on the circular iron
flying under the chef's spatula
deft turns of praise
honey lemon   sesame oil
and mongol sauce
spats that almost deafen

the party
six friends
forgetting for the moment
they're saying good-bye
yesterday and tomorrow
consumed in the succulent offering of now
wafting up six-fold from the grill
spreading across formica table
tops in blue china bowls
forever round

now
soaked with drafts
brewed for a ration of time
this irrational spell
going back for another bowl
refusing against pain
to be full

then the party rapt
by a turn of phrase
from somewhere

a ribbon of fond recognition
threads transparent through
and around them
the bond   fraternal embrace
as laughter flows

unabated
the blessed now
kissing eternity

In the Common

There you are again
on this summer night street,
your breath whispering down
from the eddies in the maples
into the marrow of my yesterdays.

These trees like old friends
sway the same way they used to
through the childhood of my wanderings,
just as the mown grass
kicks up familiar earth scents
seeped from the slicing,
and our back gate swings
with the same creaking arch,

shaping me how you made me
flesh and bone of your imaginings
with these common things
mingled in your breath. Bending back
for a draught of these old loved things,
I re-member myself with you, spirit to flesh,
and I walk again with boy's feet.

By Joe's vegetable patch I pause at
how often the earth has turned here
(and before Joe, the worms in their turn
churning hour after gritty hour,
and after old Joe, returning him under).
Stooping to sift the familiar soil
from where I've come,
I feel you again in this common,
cool ground against my palm.

Printed in the United States
892400001B